Earning with Gold

Tips on how to make profits with gold

Robert Morris

Earning with Gold

1.Introduction to Gold: history, value, and properties

Gold has always been considered a precious metal, desired and appreciated for its beauty and intrinsic value. Known since ancient times, it has been used as currency, decoration, and symbol of wealth and power. Its history is rich in charm and mystery, linked to many legends and myths that have contributed to make it even more fascinating and desirable.

Gold is one of the rarest and most precious metals on Earth. Its value is intrinsic and universal, and does not depend on external factors such as fluctuations in financial markets or political decisions. This characteristic has helped make gold a safe haven asset, a secure investment capable of preserving its value over time and protecting wealth from economic fluctuations.

But gold is not only a precious metal, it also

has extraordinary properties that make it unique and versatile. With high thermal and electrical conductivity, it is used in a variety of industrial applications, from electronics to medicine. Its resistance to corrosion makes it ideal for the production of jewelry and precious objects that maintain their beauty and brilliance over time.

Gold has an ancient and fascinating history dating back thousands of years. The earliest evidence of its processing dates back to 4000 BC, when ancient Mesopotamian and Egyptian civilizations used it to make jewelry, sacred objects, and coins. But it is with Greek and Roman civilization that gold reaches its peak of splendor, becoming a symbol of power and social status.

During the Renaissance, gold reaches another peak of splendor and sophistication, used by master goldsmiths to create jewelry and ornaments for the aristocracy and nobility. But it is with the gold rush in America during the

19th century that gold becomes a symbol of wealth and prosperity, attracting thousands of gold prospectors who set out in search of their fortune.

Today, gold is used in a variety of sectors, from the jewelry industry to the industrial sector, from dentistry to technology. With the growing demand from consumers and investors, the price of gold is subject to fluctuations and variations determined by numerous factors, such as the performance of financial markets, inflation, and geopolitics.

But despite its extraordinary characteristics and intrinsic value, gold is also one of the most controversial and criticized metals. Its extraction is often associated with environmental and social problems, such as water pollution, deforestation, and labor exploitation. Furthermore, its production and processing require the use of harmful chemicals that can damage the environment and human health.

Despite these challenges, gold remains a unique and fascinating metal, a symbol of beauty, wealth, and power. Its millennia-old history and extraordinary properties make it a precious and desired element by thousands of people around the world, who consider it a safe investment and a symbol of social status. Whether in the form of precious jewelry, gold coins, or bars, gold remains a timeless and timeless element, capable of capturing the imagination and desire of generations.

2.How to invest in gold: strategies and considerations

Investing in gold is one of the oldest and safest ways to invest. Gold has always been considered a safe haven asset, capable of protecting one's wealth in times of economic instability. But how can one invest in gold intelligently and profitably? In this article, we will explore some strategies and considerations to keep in mind for those who wish to invest in gold.

Before starting to invest in gold, it is important to understand the motivations that drive investors to choose this precious metal. One of the main reasons is its intrinsic stability. Gold is a tangible, limited asset that is universally recognized as valuable. Additionally, gold has a long history of being used as a medium of exchange and store of value, and its demand is solid and consistent over time.

Another reason to invest in gold is its ability to protect one's portfolio from inflation, deflation, and market volatility. Gold is considered a safe haven asset precisely because it tends to appreciate in times of economic and political crisis. In fact, many investors turn to gold as insurance against market uncertainty and instability.

In addition to its wealth protection function, gold can also represent an opportunity for growth and profit. Over the years, the price of gold has shown a constant upward trend, although with fluctuations due to global economic and geopolitical conditions. Investing in gold can therefore be a form of long-term investment, capable of generating attractive returns over time.

There are several ways to invest in gold, each with its own advantages and risks. The most traditional method is to purchase physical gold in the form of bars or coins. This type of investment offers the security of owning the precious metal directly, but it also involves storage and security costs. Furthermore, physical investment requires attention in choosing the gold to purchase and assessing the reliability of the seller.

An alternative to physical gold purchase is to invest in mutual funds or ETFs (Exchange Traded Funds) that track the price of gold. These financial instruments offer the flexibility and liquidity of investing in gold without having to manage the metal directly. However, it is important to keep in mind that mutual funds and ETFs involve management costs and fees that can impact investment returns.

Another option for investing in gold is trading on financial markets through futures contracts or Contracts for Difference (CFDs). These instruments allow speculating on the price of gold without physically owning it, but they also involve a higher risk due to leverage. Trading in commodities requires a good knowledge of financial markets and a well-defined investment strategy.

Finally, another way to invest in gold is through investments in sectors related to the extraction and production of the precious metal. Many mining and processing companies offer interesting investment opportunities for those who believe in the growth of the sector. However, it is important to carefully assess market conditions and the financial solidity of companies before investing.

Investing in gold offers several advantages for those looking to protect their wealth and generate attractive returns over time. However, it is crucial to carefully evaluate one's own financial needs and goals before undertaking any type of investment. Consulting a professional in the field and researching the various available options is the first step to investing in gold in an informed and profitable manner.

3. Analysis of the gold market: trends, forecasts, and influencing factors

The gold market has always been considered one of the safest and most stable financial assets, often used as a refuge in times of economic and geopolitical uncertainty. Its intrinsic characteristics make it a precious and highly sought-after asset, so much so that its price is influenced by a variety of factors ranging from the global macroeconomic context to the dynamics of financial markets. In this in-depth analysis, we will delve into the world of gold to understand current trends, future forecasts, and the main influencing factors that determine its value.

Starting with current trends, we can observe that the price of gold has been quite volatile in recent months, with significant fluctuations mainly due to the global economic situation influenced by the COVID-19 pandemic. During the most critical phase of the health crisis, gold saw an increase in its price, reaching record levels that led many investors to seek refuge in this safe haven asset. However, with the gradual improvement of the economic situation and optimism surrounding the progress of vaccination programs, the price of gold has experienced a decline, returning to more stable but still elevated levels compared to the past.

Forecasts for the future of gold are still uncertain, but many experts agree that the precious metal will continue to be a safe and valuable asset for investors seeking protection against financial market instability. The increasing demand for gold from emerging and developing countries, along with the growing presence of gold-linked ETFs, could support its price and keep it at elevated levels in the medium to long term. However, unexpected events such as a new economic crisis or an escalation of geopolitical conflicts could lead to a sudden increase in the price of gold, confirming its role as a safe haven asset.

The influencing factors that determine the price of gold are multiple and complex. Among the main factors, we can mention:

- Supply and demand: the price of gold is strongly influenced by the physical supply and demand for the precious metal, which is determined by mine production, available reserves, and demand from consumers and investors.

- Monetary policies: decisions by major issuing institutions, such as the U.S. Federal Reserve or the European Central Bank, influence the price of gold through the management of interest rates and the creation of liquidity in the financial system.

- Inflation and deflation: gold is often used as a hedge against inflation, as its value tends to increase when prices of goods and services rise. Conversely, in periods of deflation, the price of gold may decrease.

- Geopolitics: political and geopolitical events, such as wars, diplomatic crises, or instability in certain regions of the world, can influence the price of gold due to its role as a safe haven asset in times of uncertainty.

- Dollar value: gold is quoted in U.S. dollars, so its price is influenced by the value of the dollar against other currencies. A weak dollar tends to support the price of gold, while a strong dollar could lead to a decrease in its value.

In conclusion, the gold market is a complex but fascinating sector, characterized by volatile trends, uncertain forecasts, and a series of influencing factors that determine its value. Despite the uncertainties, gold remains a valuable safe haven asset for investors seeking protection against financial market and global economic instability. Carefully monitoring the price of gold and understanding its key influencing factors is essential for investors looking to seize the opportunities offered by this fascinating and timeless market.

4.Choosing the best gold investment tools: bullion, coins, ETF funds

Investing in gold is an ancient and fascinating practice that continues to attract the attention of investors worldwide. Gold is considered a safe haven asset in times of economic and political uncertainty, as it maintains its value over time and has proven to be an excellent hedge against inflation. However, deciding how to invest in gold can be a challenging task, as there are many options available on the market. Some of the most common options include gold bullion, gold coins, and ETF (Exchange-Traded Fund) funds linked to the price of gold. In this article, we will explore the characteristics of each option and discuss the pros and cons of each, to help you make an informed decision on choosing the best gold investment tools.

Gold bullion is perhaps the most traditional form of gold investment. Bullion is pieces of pure metal, usually in rectangular or square shape, minted in various sizes and weights. Gold bullion is generally considered a long-term investment, as it can be expensive to buy and sell compared to other forms of gold such as coins. However, gold bullion offers some unique advantages, such as the ability to physically own them and the potential for value appreciation over time.

One of the main reasons to invest in gold bullion is their high purity and easily recognizable standardization. Gold bullion is typically minted with a purity of 99.99%, making them a very safe option for investors seeking a stable and reliable alternative to safeguard their wealth. Additionally, gold bullion is considered a form of liquid money, as they are easily exchangeable worldwide for cash or other valuable assets.

However, there are also some disadvantages to investing in gold bullion. Firstly, gold bullion can be expensive to purchase, as the price depends on the weight and purity of the bar. Additionally, gold bullion can be difficult to sell quickly in case of need, as they require a verification and authentication process by an expert. Finally, gold bullion can be vulnerable to theft and loss, as they are physical objects that need to be stored securely.

Another common form of gold investment is gold coins. Gold coins are considered a more accessible alternative to gold bullion, as they are generally available in smaller denominations and can be bought and sold more easily. Gold coins are minted by various countries around the world and are typically aimed at collectors and investors who want to physically own their gold.

Gold coins offer several advantages over gold bullion. Firstly, gold coins are typically minted with a purity of 99.99%, making them a very safe option for investors seeking a stable and reliable alternative to safeguard their wealth. Additionally, gold coins can have added value beyond their gold content, as they can be seen as collectible items with numismatic value.

However, there are also some disadvantages to investing in gold coins. Firstly, gold coins can be subject to higher price volatility than gold bullion, as their value can be influenced by external factors such as collector demand and exchange rate fluctuations. Additionally, gold coins can be expensive to purchase, especially if you want to buy rare pieces or limited. Finally, gold coins may require more care and maintenance compared to gold bars, as they are physical objects that can wear out over time.

Finally, a modern and innovative form of investing in gold is through gold price-linked ETFs. ETFs are exchange-traded funds that track the performance of a particular index or commodity, such as gold. Investing in ETFs is considered a simpler and more convenient option compared to directly purchasing gold bars or coins, as investors can buy and sell

ETF shares on a regulated market at any time.

Gold price-linked ETFs offer several advantages over direct investments in physical gold. Firstly, ETFs offer investors the opportunity to diversify their investment portfolio without having to physically buy gold. Additionally, ETFs are considered more liquid than gold bars and coins, as ETF shares can be easily traded on the stock exchange for cash. Finally, ETFs provide investors with the opportunity to benefit from the price of gold without having to directly manage their physical gold.

However, there are also some disadvantages to investing in gold price-linked ETFs. Firstly, ETFs can be subject to higher price volatility compared to physical gold, as the value of ETF shares can be influenced by factors such as stock market fluctuations and interest rate movements. Additionally, ETFs may incur additional costs in the form of management fees and operating expenses, which can reduce the overall investment returns. Finally, ETFs do not offer investors the opportunity to physically own the underlying gold, which could be a drawback for those looking for a tangible alternative to other investment instruments.

The choice of the best gold investment tools depends on the preferences and goals of each investor. Gold bars offer a traditional and lasting form of gold investment, while gold coins can offer additional value beyond their precious metal content. Gold price-linked ETFs offer a more convenient and liquid form of gold investment, but may come with additional risks related to financial market volatility. Before making a decision, it is important to carefully evaluate the pros and cons of each option and consult a financial expert for personalized advice and guidance. With the right planning and approach, investing in gold can be an effective way to protect and grow your wealth in the long term.

5. Investing in precious gold watches

Investing in precious gold watches can bring great satisfaction from both a financial and personal perspective. Gold watches are a symbol of luxury and social status, but they are also objects of great artistic and artisanal value.

There are many reasons why investing in precious gold watches can be a advantageous decision. Firstly, gold is a precious metal with high intrinsic value that tends to hold its worth over time and resist market fluctuations. Gold watches are therefore an excellent form of safe and stable investment, which can ensure an interesting return in the long run.

Luxury gold watches are rare and sought-after items that maintain their value over time, and can even increase in value as the years go by. The rarity of some models and the particular characteristics of the materials used in their creation can significantly increase the market price of a gold watch, making it a great investment opportunity for collectors and enthusiasts in the field.

Investing in precious gold watches can also be a way to diversify one's investment portfolio, reducing the risk of losses and taking advantage of the potential appreciation of a niche market like luxury watchmaking. Furthermore, owning a prestigious gold watch can be a source of great personal satisfaction, as well as a great opportunity to wear an elegant and valuable accessory.

When investing in precious gold watches, it is important to pay attention to several factors. Firstly, it is essential to research the luxury watchmaking market and industry trends to identify the most sought-after models and those with the greatest potential for appreciation over time. It is also important to consider the authenticity and provenance of the gold watch you intend to purchase, to avoid scams and counterfeits that could compromise the value of the investment.

It is advisable to consult experts in the field and professionals in the luxury watch market to receive advice and assistance in choosing which gold watches to purchase and to evaluate the opportunity to resell the watch in the future at a higher price. Finally, it is important to take into account the additional costs associated with investing in precious gold watches, such as storage and insurance costs for the item.

Investing in precious gold watches can be a winning choice for those looking for a safe and profitable investment opportunity, as well as for those who want to own a masterpiece of craftsmanship and design to wear with pride. With the right preparation and attention to detail, it is possible to turn a simple purchase into a successful investment in the fascinating world of luxury watchmaking.

6.Gold mines: opportunities and risks in investing in mining companies

Gold mines have always represented a fascinating sector full of opportunities for investors. Gold has always played a key role as a safe-haven asset in times of economic and political uncertainty, and its demand does not seem to be decreasing in the short and medium term. Consequently, many investors are attracted to the sector of mining companies operating in gold mines, hoping to achieve significant profits.

However, investing in mining companies is not without risks. Gold mines are subject to many variables that can influence their profitability and market value. Firstly, the price of gold itself is subject to significant fluctuations on the international market, influenced by macroeconomic factors such as inflation, geopolitics, and demand from investors and end consumers. A sudden drop in the price of gold can jeopardize the economic sustainability of mining companies, which may have to face high production costs and reduced profit margins.

Furthermore, gold mines are subject to operational risks related to the complexity of extraction operations and the management of natural resources. Extracting gold is a complex and costly process that requires significant investments in equipment, technology, and skilled personnel. Mining companies must face challenges such as access to water resources, waste management, and mitigating the environmental impacts of mining activities.

Additionally, gold mines are often located in developing countries where environmental and social regulations may be less stringent than in Western countries. This leads to increased reputational risks for mining companies, which may face challenges from local communities, non-governmental organizations, and ethical investors.

Moreover, the political and economic volatility of some countries can jeopardize the safety of mining operations and access to international markets for mining companies.

Despite these risks, investing in mining companies can offer interesting opportunities for investors looking to diversify their portfolios and achieve above-average market returns. Mining companies can benefit from increases in the price of gold and realize significant profits during bullish market phases. This can result in high returns for investors who have bet on the gold mining sector.

Furthermore, mining companies offer investors the opportunity to directly participate in the real economy, contributing to the development of a country's natural resources and generating employment and wealth in local communities. Investing in mining companies can therefore have a positive impact on the economy and sustainable development of a territory, contributing to creating long-term value for shareholders and society as a whole.

To mitigate risks related to investing in mining companies, it is essential to conduct a thorough evaluation of the company and its operating context. Investors should carefully analyze the balance sheets, cash flows, and growth prospects of mining companies, also assessing the quality of management and the environmental and social sustainability of extraction activities. Additionally, it is advisable to diversify one's portfolio by investing in mining companies with diversified risk profiles and adopting risk management strategies tailored to one's investment needs.

Investing in mining companies active in gold mines can offer interesting opportunities for investors seeking above-average market returns and willing to face risks related to the volatility of the price of gold and the complexities of extraction operations. However, it is crucial to conduct thorough due diligence and adopt appropriate risk management strategies to protect one's capital and maximize long-term returns.

7. Taxes and regulations related to investing in gold

Investing in gold has always been considered one of the safest ways to protect one's wealth. Gold is a safe haven asset, an insurance against inflation and economic instability, and is considered a timeless investment that can preserve its value over time. However, before deciding to invest in gold, it is important to know the regulations and taxes related to this type of investment.

Before proceeding with a gold investment, it is important to inform yourself and consult a professional in the field to avoid costly mistakes.

One of the first things to keep in mind is that gold is considered a safe haven asset and therefore subject to different taxation compared to other types of investments. In particular, physical gold is subject to a 22%

value-added tax, while financial gold, such as certificates or funds that replicate the price of gold, is subject to ordinary taxation on capital gains, which varies depending on the taxpayer's tax regime.

Furthermore, it is important to consider that the purchase of physical gold, such as gold bars or coins, may also incur additional costs related to the storage and security of the metal. Gold is a precious asset, so it is important to store it safely, preferably in a safe or at a specialized institution, which incurs additional costs to be taken into consideration.

Regarding the sale of gold, it is important to consider that capital gains realized upon sale are subject to taxation. The taxation on capital gains varies depending on the taxpayer's tax regime and the holding period of the asset. Generally, if gold is held for less than 12 months, capital gains are treated as capital income and taxed at 26%, while if gold is held for more than 12 months, capital gains are considered capital income and taxed at 26%.

Another important aspect to consider is that investments in gold are subject to international regulations, especially concerning the possession of gold bars or coins from foreign countries. It is essential to be informed about current regulations and comply with them to avoid penalties and issues with customs authorities.

Lastly, it is important to consider that gold is a volatile asset and its price can experience significant fluctuations based on various factors, such as monetary policy, economic and geopolitical instability, and investor sentiment. Therefore, it is crucial to make a thorough assessment of risk and opportunity before deciding to invest in gold and consult an industry expert to carefully evaluate one's choices.

Investing in gold can be an interesting opportunity to diversify one's portfolio and protect one's wealth. However, it is important to be aware of the regulations and taxes related to this type of investment and consult a professional in the field before making a decision. Only in this way can one maximize earning opportunities and minimize risks associated with investing in gold.

8.Diversifying the portfolio through gold: advantages and disadvantages

When it comes to financial investments, portfolio diversification is one of the most important strategies to reduce risk and maximize returns. Among the various options available to diversify a portfolio, one of the oldest and most popular is gold. Gold has been synonymous with value and wealth for centuries and is considered a safe haven asset in times of crisis. But what are the advantages and disadvantages of investing in gold to diversify one's portfolio? In this article, we will delve into this topic, analyzing the pros and cons of this type of investment.

Let's start with the advantages. Firstly, gold is a tangible physical asset that has intrinsic value regardless of market conditions. This makes it an excellent diversification tool, as it can protect the portfolio from fluctuations and volatility in the stock and bond markets. Furthermore, gold is considered a safe haven asset, meaning a secure investment in times of economic crisis or geopolitical instability. During these periods, gold tends to appreciate, offering higher returns compared to other assets.

Another advantage of gold is its liquidity. Contrary to popular belief, gold is a highly liquid asset that can be easily bought or sold at any time. There are numerous markets and online platforms that allow investors to buy and sell gold bullion or ETFs (Exchange-Traded Funds) linked to the price of gold quickly and easily. This liquidity makes gold an attractive option for portfolio diversification without any time constraints or bureaucratic hassles.

Another positive aspect of gold is its ability to preserve purchasing power in the long term. Gold is universally recognized as a form of currency and store of value, and throughout history, it has maintained its purchasing power over time. This means that investing in gold can protect one's wealth from currency devaluation or inflation, ensuring real returns in the long run.

Finally, another advantage of gold is its scarcity and durability over time. Gold is limited in its availability and extraction, making it a rare and valuable asset. This scarcity helps maintain stable value over time, ensuring a safe and long-lasting investment.

However, investing in gold also has some disadvantages to consider. Firstly, the price of gold is influenced by numerous factors, including financial market trends, global economic conditions, monetary policies of countries, and physical supply and demand for gold. This complexity can make it difficult to predict the price of gold in the short term with certainty and can pose risks for investors.

Another disadvantage of gold is its lack of income. Unlike other financial assets, such as stocks or bonds, gold does not generate interest, dividends, or periodic cash flows. This means that investors who hold gold must rely solely on the appreciation of the gold price to earn a return on their investment. This lack of income can limit the earning potential of gold compared to other assets.

Another critical aspect of gold is its volatility. Despite being considered a safe haven asset and a secure investment, gold can be subject to significant price fluctuations in the short term. This volatility can pose risks of losses for investors who are unable to tolerate high value fluctuations in their portfolio. It is therefore important to carefully assess one's risk profile before investing in gold to diversify the portfolio.

Finally, another disadvantage of gold is its vulnerability to fraud and counterfeiting. Being a physical asset, gold is subject to the risk of counterfeiting and fraud, especially if purchased from unreliable or uncertified sources. It is important to pay attention to the origin and authenticity of the gold purchased to avoid falling victim to scams or fakes.

In conclusion, investing in gold to diversify your portfolio can be a valid strategy to protect your wealth and achieve stable returns in the long term. However, it is important to carefully evaluate the advantages and disadvantages of this type of investment and consider your risk profile before making a decision. Consulting a finance expert and conducting thorough research on the gold market are crucial steps to ensure making an informed and secure investment.

9. How to Monitor and Manage Your Gold Investment

Investing in gold is one of the most popular options for those looking to protect their wealth and diversify their portfolio. However, it is important to carefully monitor and manage your gold investment to maximize returns and protect your interests.

The first step to monitor and manage your gold investment is understanding the factors that influence the price of gold. Gold prices are influenced by various factors, including market demand and supply, interest rates, inflation, economic and geopolitical stability, and movements of the dollar. It is important to constantly monitor these factors to make informed decisions about your investment.

Another important step is choosing the best way to invest in gold. There are several options available for investing in gold, including buying physical gold bars, investing in gold mutual funds, buying shares of gold mining companies, and purchasing gold through futures and options contracts. It is important to evaluate the different options and choose the one that best suits your investment needs and goals.

Once you have chosen your gold investment option, it is important to constantly monitor the price of gold and market trends. It is advisable to use technical and fundamental analysis tools to assess growth prospects and potential investment opportunities. It is also important to be aware of gold price fluctuations and act accordingly to protect your investment.

Furthermore, it is important to diversify your gold investment portfolio to reduce the risk of losses. It is advisable to diversify your gold investment through the purchase of different types of assets, such as physical gold bars, shares of gold mining companies, and gold mutual funds. This way, the risk of losses due to poor performance of a single asset is reduced.

Finally, it is important to be aware of the taxes and expenses associated with gold investment. It is important to evaluate potential taxes and fees to ensure that your investment returns are not eroded by high costs and commissions. It is also advisable to consult with an experienced financial advisor for personalized advice and support in managing your gold investment.

Carefully monitoring and managing your gold investment is essential to maximize returns and protect your wealth. It is important to be aware of the factors influencing the price of gold, choose the best way to invest in gold, constantly monitor the market, diversify your gold investment portfolio, and manage the taxes and expenses associated with the investment. By following these steps, you can protect and grow your gold investment in the long run.

Investing in gold is one of the most popular strategies for diversifying investment portfolios. However, like any other type of investment, it is important to carefully assess risk and manage potential losses to protect invested capital. In this article, we will provide advice on how to assess risk and manage losses when investing in gold.

First and foremost, it is important to understand that gold is considered a safe haven asset in times of economic and political uncertainty. As a result, the price of gold is influenced by a variety of factors, including inflation, market volatility, and international geopolitical situations. Therefore, it is crucial to carefully evaluate these factors before deciding to invest in gold.

One of the first steps to assess risk is to conduct a thorough analysis of gold market trends. It is important to monitor the price of gold in the short and long term, as well as consider expert forecasts in the field. Additionally, studying the historical behavior of gold in times of crisis and economic stability can help understand how it may react in different situations.

Another aspect to consider is the amount of gold to purchase. Typically, experts recommend allocating a small portion of your investment portfolio to gold to diversify risk. Additionally, it is important to decide whether to buy physical gold or invest in exchange-traded funds (ETFs).

The text translated into English is:

"related to the price of gold. Both options have advantages and disadvantages, so it is important to carefully evaluate which solution is most suitable for your needs.

Once the investment in gold has been made, it is important to constantly monitor the market trends to be ready to react in case of losses. In the event of significant variations in the price of gold, it is advisable to consider whether it is appropriate to sell part or all of the investment to limit losses. Alternatively, risk hedging strategies can be adopted, such as using futures contracts or options on gold.

Finally, it is essential to create a risk management plan to protect the capital invested in gold. This plan should include clear investment objectives, loss limits that must not be exceeded, and exit strategies in the event of significant price fluctuations in gold. Additionally, it is important to diversify the investment portfolio to reduce overall risk.

In conclusion, investing in gold can be a profitable strategy to diversify the investment portfolio. However, it is essential to carefully assess the risk and manage losses prudently to protect the capital invested. By following the advice provided in this article and adopting a solid risk management strategy, it is possible to maximize returns and protect investments in gold."

10. How to sell gold: tips on when and how to monetize your investment

Gold has always been considered a safe asset to invest in, as its value tends to grow over time and can provide protection against inflation and economic instability. However, at the right time, it is important to know how to monetize your investment in gold to maximize your profit. In this article, we will provide tips on when and how to sell gold to maximize your earnings.

The ideal time to sell gold depends on several factors, including the global gold market, economic trends, and personal financial conditions. Generally, it is advisable to sell gold when the following factors occur:

1. High prices: monitoring gold prices on the global market constantly is essential to understand when is the best time to sell. If gold prices are high, you could make a higher

profit from selling your investment.

2. Financial need: if you need immediate liquidity to cover unexpected expenses or to invest in other financial opportunities, it might be the right time to sell gold.

3. Changes in the economy: during periods of economic instability or political turbulence, the price of gold tends to increase. Therefore, you may want to consider selling your investment during such periods to maximize your profit.

Once you have decided to sell your gold, it is important to know the available options and choose the most suitable method to maximize your earnings. Here are some tips on how to monetize your investment in gold:

1. Sell physical gold: if you own jewelry, coins, or gold bars, you can sell them directly

to a precious metals dealer or a gold refinery. Before selling, make sure to get evaluations from multiple buyers to ensure you get the best possible price.

2. Use online services: there are numerous online services that allow you to sell gold quickly and conveniently. However, it is important to be careful to choose a reliable and reputable provider to avoid scams or fraud.

3. Gold trading: if you are an experienced investor, you may consider trading gold on the commodities market. This method can offer the opportunity to make high profits, but it is important to be aware of the risks associated with trading.

4. Invest in gold funds: if you do not want to physically manage gold, you can invest in exchange-traded funds (ETFs) or mutual funds that track the price of gold. This method

allows you to benefit from the gold market without physically owning gold.

Regardless of the method chosen to sell gold, it is advisable to keep in mind some tips to maximize your earnings:

1. Do thorough research: before selling gold, it is essential to educate yourself about the gold market, current prices, and market trends. It is also advisable to get evaluations from multiple buyers to ensure you get the best price possible.

2. Evaluate the fees and expenses: when selling gold, make sure to consider all the commissions and associated expenses, such as transfer fees and management fees. These costs can impact your final profit, so it is important to take them into consideration.

3. Keep documentation: make sure to keep all

documents related to the sale of gold, including receipts, contracts, and communications with the buyer. This will help you track the transaction and resolve any disputes in the future.

4. Consult a professional: if you are unsure about how to proceed with selling your gold, it is advisable to consult a financial expert or industry professional. A qualified consultant can help you make informed decisions and maximize your earnings.

Monetizing your gold investment can be an opportunity to obtain significant profit. With the right strategy and proper planning, you can maximize your earnings and get the most value from your gold investment. By following the advice provided in this article and paying attention to details, you can sell gold efficiently and profitably.

11. Gold Geology: How It Forms and Where It's Generally Found

Gold is one of the most precious metals in the world and has fascinated humanity since ancient times for its rarity, brilliance, and durability. Gold geology is a fascinating field of study that seeks to understand how this metal forms and where it is most likely to be found.

Gold primarily forms in two ways: through primary processes related to the formation of igneous rocks and through secondary processes related to the deposition of mineral solution in areas rich in water and gas.

In primary formation, gold is often found associated with igneous rocks, such as granite and quartz, which have formed from the solidification of magma below the Earth's surface. During magma cooling and crystallization, gold and other minerals concentrate in the cracks and cavities of rocks, forming gold veins that can be extracted through mining techniques.

In secondary formation, gold is often found associated with alluvial deposits, such as rivers and placers. In this case, gold forms through dissolution and recrystallization in mineral solutions rich in water and gas that infiltrate rocks and sediments. Over time, these deposits concentrate in areas of high water flow, forming gold seams that can be easily collected through alluvial extraction techniques.

In general, gold is found in small quantities in the Earth's crust, with an average concentration of about 0.005 parts per million. However, in some areas of the world, such as South Africa, Australia, the United States, Canada, and Russia, much richer gold deposits are found, making these regions some of the most important gold producers globally.

Modern prospecting and mining techniques have led to the discovery of new gold deposits in locations previously thought unsuitable for its presence, such as active volcanic areas, underwater regions, or even outer space. These discoveries have significantly expanded global gold reserves and have helped to keep demand for this precious metal high.

Gold geology is a complex and fascinating field that seeks to understand how this metal forms and where it is most likely to be found. Through centuries of studies and research, many of the main sources of gold have been identified, and advanced techniques have been developed for its efficient and sustainable extraction. Thanks to this knowledge, gold has continued to maintain its intrinsic value and economic importance in the modern world.

12. Tools and equipment necessary for gold prospecting

Gold prospecting is a fascinating activity but it requires the use of specific tools and equipment to be carried out efficiently and safely. Here is a detailed list of all the tools and equipment necessary for gold prospecting.

1. Boat: If you intend to search for gold in rivers or lakes, it is necessary to have a boat to reach the most remote and inaccessible areas from the shores.

2. Shovel: The shovel is a fundamental tool for digging the earth and sediment in search of gold nuggets. It is advisable to opt for a sturdy and good quality shovel to avoid breakages during the search.

3. Sieve: The sieve is an essential tool for separating gold from the earth and inert

material. There are sieves of different types and sizes, to adapt to the different research needs.

4. Tweezers: Tweezers are useful for collecting gold nuggets and smaller fragments without touching them directly with hands.

5. Suction pipette: The suction pipette is an indispensable tool for suctioning gold from sediments and waste materials without risking losing it.

6. Mouth guards and masks: During gold prospecting, it is important to protect the respiratory tract from fumes and harmful dust that may be emitted during the activity. For this reason, it is advisable to use mouth guards and protective masks.

7. Gloves: Gloves are useful for protecting hands during gold prospecting, avoiding

possible injuries and irritations caused by abrasive materials.

8. Magnetic can opener: The magnetic can opener is a tool used to collect magnetic gold present in sediments and waste materials.

9. Headlamp: To allow greater visibility during research activities, it is advisable to use a headlamp to fix on the head.

10. Object basket: To keep all the tools and equipment necessary for gold prospecting in order and safe, it is advisable to use a sturdy and spacious object basket.

11. Pickaxes: Pickaxes are used to break the hardest and most complex rocks in search of gold nuggets.

12. Pans: Pans are used to separate gold from

sand and sediments, allowing to highlight the presence of nuggets and precious fragments.

13. Tool carrying backpack: To comfortably transport all the tools and equipment necessary for gold prospecting, it is advisable to use a sturdy and spacious tool carrying backpack.

14. Compass and map: To orient oneself during excursions in search of gold, it is essential to have a compass and a detailed map of the territory.

15. Bag for collecting gold: Bags are used to safely and neatly store the gold collected during research activities.

16. Washing tables: Washing tables are used to separate gold from sediments using the technique of washing with running water.

Gold prospecting is an activity that requires the use of specific tools and equipment to be carried out efficiently and safely. It is advisable to invest in good quality materials suitable for one's needs to achieve the best results during research activities.

13. Finding gold in rivers and in the ground

The search for gold in rivers and in the ground has fascinated humanity since ancient times. Gold has always been considered a precious metal, a symbol of wealth and power, and its discovery has often led to fortune and prosperity for those who have found it.

The search for gold is an activity that requires patience, determination, and specific knowledge. In fact, it is not enough to know where to look, but it is essential to know the techniques and tools necessary to identify and extract gold effectively and safely.

Rivers are one of the main sources where gold can be found, as the precious metal is carried by the water and deposited on the bottom due to its high density. To identify gold in rivers, it is necessary to use equipment such as a sieve for sand and gravel, a bowl for washing the extracted material, and a metal detector to identify deeper deposits. Additionally, it is important to know the geological and topographical characteristics of the area where you intend to search, as the presence of rock formations and other terrain features can influence the presence and concentration of gold.

Another widespread technique for searching for gold in rivers is the technique of "panning", which involves filling a bowl with sand and gravel from the riverbed and shaking it gently to bring out the gold, which remains at the bottom of the bowl. This technique requires a lot of practice and skill, but it can be very effective in identifying small gold nuggets in rivers.

In addition to rivers, it is possible to search for gold in the ground. This activity is known as dry prospecting and is very common in many regions of the world. To find gold in the ground, various techniques can be used, such as searching with a metal detector, which allows the presence of metals in the ground to be identified exploiting variations in the earth's magnetic field. In addition, the technique of "dry-washing" can be used, which involves sifting the ground and using a fan to separate the gold from lighter materials.

In addition to techniques and tools, it is essential to have a good knowledge of gold deposits and areas where gold is most likely to be found. For example, alluvial deposits, formed by sand and gravel transported by rivers, are often rich in gold, while other areas may be poorer in minerals. Moreover, it is important to consider local regulations and obtain the necessary permits before starting the search for gold, to avoid incurring penalties and fines.

The search for gold in rivers and in the ground is a fascinating and exciting activity that requires commitment and dedication, but can bring great satisfaction both economically and personally. However, it is important to remember that the search for gold can also be a dangerous activity, especially if safety regulations are not followed and the risks associated with mineral extraction are underestimated. Therefore, it is essential to always be careful and cautious during the search for gold, to avoid accidents and safeguard one's safety.

The search for gold in rivers and in the ground is a fascinating activity that requires specific knowledge, appropriate equipment, and above all patience and determination. With the right preparation and necessary effort, it is possible to identify and extract gold effectively and safely, achieving satisfaction and tangible results. However, it is important to always act in respect of the environment and safety regulations, to avoid damage and dangers during the gold search activity.

14. Gold extraction in rivers

Gold extraction in rivers is an ancient practice that has involved many civilizations over the centuries. Gold is extracted from river beds and sediments through a series of techniques that vary depending on the amount of gold present and the geology of the surrounding terrain. Over time, various methodologies have been developed to extract gold efficiently and sustainably.

One of the most common techniques for gold extraction in rivers is the so-called "panning", which involves using a "gold pan" or gold bowl to collect river sediments and separate gold from sand and mud. This technique requires a certain skill and patience, as it is necessary to move the bowl in a way that separates the gold from the remaining sand in order to gradually wash away the debris. The heavier gold settles at the bottom of the bowl, while lighter debris is washed away with water.

Another commonly used technique for gold extraction in rivers is "sluicing", which involves using a "sluice box" or sediment box. This box is usually placed along the river so that water flows through it carrying sediments and gold. Inside the sluice box are grids that capture the gold while water flows away. The gold settles at the bottom of the box along with other heavier debris, allowing extractors to recover the gold more efficiently than panning.

Other techniques for gold extraction in rivers include the use of dredges, which are machines used to dig up the river bed and collect large amounts of sand and sediments that are then sifted to find gold. Dredges can be manual or motorized and require a certain level of knowledge and skill to be used effectively.

It is important to note that gold extraction in

rivers can pose environmental problems, as the techniques used can cause water contamination and destroy the surrounding natural environments. Therefore, it is essential to adopt sustainable and responsible practices to minimize environmental impact and protect the biodiversity of rivers.

Finally, it is important to emphasize that gold extraction in rivers is a regulated activity in many countries and requires the necessary permits to be carried out legally. It is therefore essential to respect current environmental laws and regulations to avoid sanctions and protect the surrounding environment.

15.Extraction Techniques of Gold in the Earth

The extraction of gold from the earth is a complex process that requires a wide use of specialized techniques and machinery. Mining activities for gold extraction can be divided into two main categories: open-pit mining and underground mining.

Open-pit mining is generally used when the ore reserves are very extensive and the gold concentration is relatively low. In this case, the earth is removed to expose the underlying gold ore. Once the ore is extracted, it is crushed and ground to reduce it into small pieces that can be treated through various processes such as cyanidation, gravity separation, and flotation.

Cyanidation is one of the most commonly used methods for open-pit gold extraction. This process involves the use of cyanide to dissolve gold from the ore. The ground ore is mixed with a cyanide solution and the gold is then extracted into solution. This solution is then subjected to purification processes to obtain pure gold.

Gravity separation is another process used for open-pit gold extraction. This method relies on the difference in specific weight between gold and other materials present in the ore. The ore is passed through a series of separators that use gravity to separate gold from other materials. Once separated, the gold can be melted and refined to obtain pure gold.

Flotation is another method used for open-pit gold extraction. This process involves the use of chemicals that bond to gold and make it float, allowing it to be separated from other materials present in the ore. Once separated, the gold is isolated and refined to obtain pure gold.

On the other hand, underground mining is used when the ore reserves are smaller and the gold concentration is higher. In this case, miners descend into the mines to extract the gold ore. Mines can be excavated using various techniques, including tunnels and extraction shafts.

Once the ore is extracted, it is transported to the surface to be treated and separated from the gold. Cyanidation, gravity separation, and flotation processes are commonly used for underground gold extraction as well. However, underground mining can be more dangerous and requires a higher level of attention and specific skills from miners.

In both cases, the extraction of gold from the earth requires great attention to the environment and the safety of workers. The use of chemicals such as cyanide can be extremely harmful to the environment if not managed properly. It is therefore essential to adopt adequate safety measures and constantly monitor the impact of mining activities on the surrounding environment.

The extraction of gold from the earth is a complex process that requires the use of specialized techniques and machinery. Mining activities can be conducted both in open-pit and underground mines, and the extraction process may vary depending on the characteristics of the gold ore. Ensuring the safety and sustainability of mining activities is crucial to preserve the environment and ensure the well-being of the workers involved.

16. Techniques for cleaning and refining gold

Gold is a very valuable metal, and for this reason, its cleaning and refining must be carried out with extreme care and precision to ensure its quality and value. There are various techniques used to separate gold from other impurities and to make it shiny and pure.

The first step in cleaning and refining gold is the separation of minerals and impurities that are found together with the precious metal. This process is called extraction and can be done through both manual and industrial methods. Among the most common methods is gravity separation, which exploits the different density of gold compared to other materials present in the rock or ore.

Once separated, gold is then subjected to various purification processes to ensure its maximum quality. One of the most common processes is chemical refining, which uses chemicals such as acids and reagents to remove impurities from raw gold. This process is very delicate and requires the use of specialized equipment and knowledge of the chemical properties of gold.

Another method used for the purification of gold is electrolysis, which exploits the electrical conductivity of the metal to separate it from impurities through an electrolysis process. This method is very precise and allows for obtaining gold of very high purity, suitable for use in jewelry or other sectors that require a high-quality product.

Once the gold has been purified, it can be plated or worked to obtain the desired shape. This process can be carried out through techniques such as rolling, melting, or molding, depending on the characteristics of the gold and the desired end result. For example, if one wishes to obtain a pure gold ingot, the molten gold can be poured into a mold and allowed to cool to solidify.

Finally, gold can be polished to make it shiny and sparkling. This process can be done manually using specific polishing pastes or through specialized machinery that uses ultrasonic vibrations or other methods to achieve an optimal result.

In conclusion, the cleaning and refining of gold are complex and delicate processes that require specialized skills and specific equipment. However, thanks to these techniques, it is possible to obtain gold of very high quality and value, which can be used in various sectors such as jewelry, electronics, or coin production.

17. Where to find Silver

In addition to gold, there are other precious metals such as silver. Silver is a highly sought-after precious metal for the production of jewelry, coins, silverware, and other artifacts. Its shine and resistance to corrosion make it a highly valued material in the industry and jewelry sector. But where can silver be found? And what are its main sources?

Silver is a chemical element found in nature, although in limited quantities compared to other metals such as gold and copper. It is mainly found in the form of silver-bearing minerals, which are rocks that contain a significant concentration of silver. There are several areas in the world where silver deposits can be found, each with its own characteristics and peculiarities.

One of the countries richest in silver is

Mexico, which boasts numerous silver mines among the most productive in the world. The Fresnillo mine, located in the state of Zacatecas, is one of the largest and most important, with an annual production of over 40 million ounces of silver. Peru is also a major producer of silver, with mines like Cannatue and Colquijirca making significant contributions to global production.

Other regions of the world where important silver deposits can be found include Australia, Chile, China, and Argentina. Each country has its own techniques for extracting and processing silver, which can vary depending on the geological characteristics of the deposits and the available resources.

One of the most common techniques for extracting silver is the amalgam extraction, which involves the use of mercury to separate silver from the rest of the ore. This method, if not managed properly, can pose risks to the environment and human health, as mercury is a toxic metal. For this reason, many silver mines are looking to adopt more sustainable and eco-friendly solutions for metal extraction.

In addition to mining production, silver can also be extracted from recycled materials such as old jewelry, coins, or silver artifacts. This recycling process is important both to reduce the consumption of natural resources and to minimize the environmental impact associated with mining extraction.

One of the most common sources of recycled silver is old photographic films, which contain a significant amount of silver used in image production. With the transition to digital photography, the amount of silver derived from this sector has decreased, but it still represents an important source of recovery for this precious metal.

In addition to the production of jewelry and

silverware, silver is also used in other sectors of the industry such as electronics, medicine, and mirror production. Its electrical and thermal conductivity make it an ideal material for the production of electronic circuits, sensors, and medical devices.

Silver is a highly valued precious metal for its aesthetic and functional qualities. Its extraction mainly occurs through silver mines scattered around the world, as well as through the recycling of silver-containing materials. This precious metal plays an important role in various industries and production sectors, contributing to the creation of high-quality and valuable artifacts.

18. Where to Find Platinum: It is a rare and precious metal, often used for high-quality jewelry

Platinum is a very rare precious metal, with unique chemical and physical characteristics that make it particularly suitable for specialized uses, such as in the production of high-quality jewelry, scientific instruments, and electronic components. Its rarity and properties make it very expensive and highly sought after on the international market.

Platinum is found in nature primarily in platinum mineral deposits, which form in specific geological environments and are often associated with other rocks and metals. The major platinum-producing countries are South Africa, Russia, Canada, and Zimbabwe, which together cover most of the global production of this precious metal.

In South Africa, platinum is mainly extracted

from the platinum mineral deposits in the Bushveld Complex, a vast geological region rich in platinum minerals. Some of the largest and most productive platinum mines in the world, such as the Impala Mine and the Stillwater Mine, are located here.

In Russia, platinum is mainly extracted from the southern Siberian region, where there are rich platinum mineral deposits associated with ultrabasic and basaltic rocks. The Norilsk and Kondyor mines are among the most important in the country and provide a significant amount of platinum to the global market.

In Canada, platinum is primarily extracted from the Sudbury region in Ontario, where there are significant platinum mineral deposits associated with volcanic rocks. The Sudbury and Thunder Bay mines are among the largest and most productive in the country and play a significant role in the international platinum market.

In Zimbabwe, platinum is mainly extracted from the Great Dyke region, a long geological structure rich in platinum minerals associated with intrusive rocks. The Mimosa and Ngezi mines are among the most important in the country and provide a significant portion of global platinum production.

In addition to the major platinum-producing countries, there are also other states that have significant reserves of this precious metal, such as the United States, Australia, Brazil, and Botswana. However, platinum production in these countries is generally lower compared to those mentioned earlier.

Since platinum is a rare and precious metal, its extraction and processing require specialized and expensive techniques, which make its production cost very high. This contributes to its high value on the international market and its popularity among producers of high-quality jewelry and other industrial sectors that require durable and resistant materials.

Platinum is a very rare and precious metal primarily found in a few countries around the world, such as South Africa, Russia, Canada, and Zimbabwe. Its extraction is a complex and costly process, but the benefits of its use in various industrial sectors, such as high-quality jewelry, are undeniable. Due to its unique properties and rarity, platinum remains one of the most coveted and appreciated metals in the global market.

Platinum is a rare and precious metal used in various sectors such as the automotive industry, jewelry, electronics, and the chemical industry. Its rarity and value make it a highly sought-after metal, and finding platinum in rivers can be a very profitable activity for those who manage to find it.

To find platinum in rivers, it is necessary to have basic knowledge of geology and mineralogy, as well as appropriate equipment to uncover platinum deposits. Platinum is often found associated with minerals such as pyrite, magnetite, and quartz, so it is important to know how to recognize and locate them.

One of the best places to search for platinum in rivers is alluvial deposits, which are sediments that settle on the riverbed as a result of debris and material transported by water. These sediments may contain traces of platinum from the underlying rocks, making them an excellent starting point for the search.

To identify alluvial deposits, it is advisable to inspect the riverbed for dark and heavy sediments, which may indicate the presence of minerals such as pyrite and magnetite, generally associated with platinum. Additionally, a metal detector can be used to detect any traces of platinum in the surrounding area.

Once alluvial deposits are identified, collecting the material can be done using sieves and washing to separate the platinum from sand and mud. It is important to pay attention to the presence of magnetic minerals, which may indicate the presence of platinum, and use specific equipment to capture the heavier particles.

It is important to emphasize that searching for platinum in rivers can be a tiring and demanding activity that requires time and patience. Additionally, it is necessary to adhere to local regulations regarding mining extraction and environmental protection to avoid damage to the flora and fauna in rivers.

To find platinum in rivers, it is advisable to research the geological characteristics of the area of interest, consult geological maps, and seek advice from industry experts. Furthermore, participating in specific training courses on the search for precious minerals in rivers can provide the necessary skills to successfully conduct this activity.

Searching for platinum in rivers can be a fascinating and rewarding activity for those who love geology and mineralogy, and can be a great source of income for those who can identify platinum deposits and extract it properly and responsibly. With the right preparation and equipment, it is possible to find platinum in rivers and enjoy the benefits of this precious metal.

19. Where to Find Rhodium

Rhodium is a precious metal belonging to the platinum group and is known for its brightness and resistance to corrosion. It is highly sought after for its ability to protect and coat precious jewelry, as well as for its utility in the production of car catalysts and various industrial sectors.

For anyone interested in purchasing rhodium, there are several options to consider. First and foremost, it is important to keep in mind that rhodium is a rare and precious metal, so its price can vary significantly based on market demand and supply. This is why it may be necessary to do thorough research to find the best available price.

One of the main sources to purchase rhodium is specialized auction houses for precious metals. These auction houses regularly offer the opportunity to participate in auctions where you can buy rhodium ingots of various sizes and purities. It is important to pay attention to the sales conditions, commissions, and shipping costs, which can influence the final cost of the metal.

Another option to purchase rhodium is through suppliers specialized in the trade of precious metals. These suppliers can offer high-quality rhodium ingots at competitive prices, ensuring the security of the transaction and the fast and secure delivery of the purchased metal. It is advisable to look for reliable and reputable suppliers to avoid risks or scams.

Furthermore, it is possible to purchase rhodium through financial intermediaries specializing in the trade of precious metals. These intermediaries offer simple and convenient investment solutions to buy and hold rhodium in the form of futures contracts or exchange-traded funds. This option is particularly suitable for those looking to invest in rhodium for long-term returns, although it carries risks associated with market volatility.

Those who prefer to buy rhodium in the form of jewelry or art objects can turn to jewelers specialized in the processing of precious metals. These jewelers can offer custom and personalized creations made with rhodium, ensuring the quality and authenticity of the metal used. Additionally, rhodium can be found in luxury jewelry stores and specialized boutiques, where unique and refined jewelry made with rhodium and other precious metals are displayed.

In conclusion, rhodium is a precious metal with numerous applications and possibilities that can be found in various forms and outlets. It is important to conduct detailed research and carefully evaluate the available options to choose the most suitable source according to one's needs and preferences. Purchasing rhodium can be a safe and profitable investment, as long as the risks and opportunities offered by the precious metals market are taken into consideration.

20. Where to Find Ruthenium

Ruthenium is a transition metal belonging to the platinum group in the periodic table of elements. It is a hard, white-silvery metal, resistant to corrosion and with a high melting point. Its presence in the Earth's crust is rather limited, but it can be found in nature in the form of lead and copper minerals. However, its concentration is very low, making it difficult and expensive to extract in significant quantities.

Ruthenium is mainly extracted as a byproduct of platinum, palladium, and iridium processing. These metals are often found together in nickel, copper, and lead mineral deposits. The extraction process for ruthenium involves separating it from other metals through a series of complex refining and purification operations.

One of the main producers of ruthenium is

Russia, which holds large reserves of platinum and palladium and primarily extracts ruthenium as a byproduct of these mining activities. South Africa is also a major producer of ruthenium, thanks to its rich platinum and palladium deposits.

If one wishes to find ruthenium for scientific or industrial purposes, it can be purchased on the commodities market. There are several companies specialized in selling pure ruthenium or ruthenium alloys with other metals. These companies provide the metal in various forms, such as powder, wires, bars, or sheets, depending on the customer's needs.

Another alternative source to obtain ruthenium is through recycling electronic components and spent catalysts. Ruthenium is often used in these devices for its corrosion resistance and high temperature properties. By collecting and recycling these materials, it is possible to recover ruthenium and reduce dependence on primary extraction sources.

However, it is important to note that ruthenium is a rare and precious metal, with a high price due to its limited availability and the complexity of its extraction and production process.

Ruthenium is a valuable and rare transition metal that can mainly be found as a byproduct of platinum and palladium processing. Ruthenium can be purchased on the commodities market or obtained through recycling electronic components and spent catalysts. Due to its limited availability and high price, ruthenium is considered a niche metal used primarily in high-tech applications and specialized industries.

21. Where to find Iridium

Iridium is a very rare and precious metal, belonging to the transition metals group. It is found in nature mainly in the form of an alloy with platinum, called iridosmine. This metal was discovered in 1803 by Smithson Tennant, a British chemist and scientist. It was named iridium from the Latin "iris," which means rainbow, for the vibrant colors it takes on when oxidized.

Iridium is mainly found in nature in platinum mineral deposits, such as pentlandite and sperrylite. These deposits are often located in volcanic regions or in river placers, where sediments from platinum-containing rocks are transported and deposited by water. Iridium deposits are very rare and scattered worldwide, with the main extraction areas located in South Africa, Russia, Canada, and Alaska. Most of the extracted iridium is used in industry and manufacturing techniques, thanks to its unique physical and chemical properties. Iridium is known for its resistance to corrosion, temperature, and wear, and is widely used in the production of electrodes for chlorine production and in the manufacturing of surgical tools and laboratory instruments. Additionally, iridium is an important material for the production of high-quality jewelry, thanks to its luster and scratch resistance.

To find iridium in nature, it is necessary to follow specific steps. Firstly, one can search for information on platinum mineral deposits in regions known for the presence of iridium. This information can be found on specialized geological websites, geology books, and mineralogical maps. Additionally, consulting mining industry experts for advice and guidance on where to look can be helpful. Once a promising area is identified, it is important to procure the necessary equipment for searching for iridium. This equipment includes pickaxes, sieves, drills, and other mining tools. It is also advisable to wear weather-resistant and shock-resistant clothing to protect oneself during the search.

Searching for iridium can be a long and exhausting process, as it requires digging and sifting through large amounts of soil to find even a small amount of metal. It is important to pay attention to signs indicating the presence of iridium, such as the presence of platinum mineral samples, metallic colors in the rock, or heavy materials in the sieve.

Once iridium is found, extraction and processing can be carried out. This can be done through the use of chemical and metallurgical processes, which allow for the separation of iridium from platinum minerals and purification. Once pure iridium is obtained, it can be used for the production of jewelry, laboratory instruments, or other industrial applications.

In conclusion, iridium is a rare and precious metal found mainly in platinum mineral deposits worldwide. To find it, specific steps must be followed and specialized equipment must be used. Once found, iridium can be extracted and processed for use in various industrial and artisanal applications.

22. Where to find Osmium

Osmium is a transition metal that is primarily found in nature combined with other metals such as iridium, platinum, ruthenium, and palladium. It is considered one of the rarest metals on Earth and is mainly used in industrial and scientific applications.

To find osmium, one must go to specific places where it is extracted as a by-product of platinum and other metal mines. Some of the main osmium-producing regions include South Africa, Russia, Canada, and the United States.

In particular, South Africa is the world's leading producer of osmium, as it is rich in platinum deposits and other platinum group metals where osmium is present in significant quantities. The platinum mines located in the Bushveld Complex region in South Africa are among the most important sources of osmium on Earth.

Outside of South Africa, osmium can also be found in Russia, particularly in the Noril'sk region, where nickel and ruthenium deposits containing traces of osmium are found. In Canada, platinum mines located in the Sudbury region in Ontario are another important source of osmium.

In the United States, osmium can be mainly extracted from platinum mines located in Alaska and Montana. However, the United States is not among the main producers of osmium worldwide, with relatively limited production compared to other countries.

To find osmium in nature, one must therefore look to these specific regions where the metal is present in significant quantities. Platinum mines and other platinum group metals are the main sources of osmium, so it is important to choose locations where such extraction activities are present.

Once osmium is found, it can be used for a variety of industrial and scientific applications. Osmium is known for its high density, high melting point, and corrosion resistance, making it ideal for use in jewelry, surgical instruments, electronic components, and chemical catalysts.

In terms of commercial availability, osmium can be purchased from specialized suppliers of rare and high-purity metals. Osmium can be found in the form of powder, granules, or ingots, depending on the needs and intended uses.

In conclusion, osmium is a precious and rare metal that can be found mainly in platinum mines and other platinum group metals. Regions such as South Africa, Russia, Canada, and the United States are among the main sources of osmium in nature, so it is important to look to these areas to find this particular metal. Once extracted, osmium can be used in a variety of industrial and scientific sectors, offering a unique and valuable presence in the world of metals.

23. Where to find Palladium

Palladium, also known as native palladium, is a rare and precious mineral belonging to the transition metals class. Its name comes from Palladio, a Greek deity who personified Divine Wisdom and was associated with the protection of miners. Palladium is very similar to platinum, but is lighter and less dense. It is a ductile, malleable, and corrosion-resistant metal, characteristics that make it highly valued in the automotive, chemical, and jewelry industries.

Palladium is primarily found in nature in small quantities, often associated with deposits of platinum, nickel, and copper. Its presence has been identified in various parts of the world, but the main producing countries are Russia, Canada, the United States, South Africa, and Brazil. Palladium deposits also contain other minerals, such as cerite, britholite, loparite, and brass.

For those who wish to find Palladium, it is important to know that its extraction is a complex and expensive activity that requires the use of specialized equipment and knowledge of specific processing techniques. Generally, Palladium is extracted from primary or secondary deposits, where it is found associated with other minerals. Primary deposits are those where Palladium is found in its native form, while secondary deposits are those where it is found in sulfides or oxides.

One of the most famous places in the world to find Palladium is Siberia, particularly the Norilsk region, where some of the richest deposits of this metal are located. In Russia, Palladium is mainly extracted from the Norilsk Nickel mines, one of the world's leading producers of precious metals. In Canada, Palladium is mainly found in the Stillwater mines in Ontario, and Lac des Iles mines in Manitoba.

In the United States, California is one of the places where Palladium can be found, particularly in the Los Angeles region where some active mines are located. In Africa, South Africa is one of the world's main producers of Palladium, with deposits mainly located in the Transvaal region.

Palladium can also be found in Brazil, particularly in the Minas Gerais region where some of the most important deposits of this metal are located. Brazilian Palladium deposits also contain other precious minerals such as gold, silver, and platinum.

For those who wish to find Palladium in nature, it is important to keep in mind that the extraction of this metal is a complex and regulated activity that requires compliance with strict environmental and safety regulations. It is therefore essential to inform oneself about local laws and regulations before undertaking any extraction activities.

Furthermore, it is important to carefully assess the costs and risks associated with Palladium extraction, which can be a very costly and dangerous activity. It is advisable to rely on industry professionals and follow the guidance of expert geologists and mining engineers to maximize the chances of success.

Palladium is a rare and precious mineral found in various countries around the world, mainly in Russia, Canada, the United States, South Africa, and Brazil. Its extraction is a complex and regulated activity that requires specialized equipment, technical knowledge, and compliance with environmental and safety regulations. Those who wish to find Palladium must therefore inform themselves carefully and rely on industry professionals to maximize the chances of success.

24. Where to find Rhenium

Rhenium is a very rare chemical element that is found in nature in very limited quantities. It is mainly present as a byproduct of molybdenum and copper extraction, but it is difficult to find in pure forms. The main problem in searching for this element is that it is very expensive to extract and purify, so it is not easily available on the market.

A common source of rhenium is the mineral molybdenite, which is mainly composed of molybdenum but can also contain variable amounts of rhenium. However, the concentration of rhenium in this mineral is generally very low, around 0.02%. This means that large quantities of ore need to be extracted and treated to obtain significant amounts of rhenium.

Other sources of rhenium include copper deposits, where it is generally found in higher concentrations compared to molybdenum ore. However, in this case too, it is necessary to separate rhenium from other metals present in the ore, which can be a complex and costly process.

Another possible source of rhenium is in nuclear reactors, where it is produced as a byproduct of uranium nuclear fission. However, this source is very limited and the rhenium produced in this way is generally intended for specific uses in the aerospace and nuclear medicine industries.

Since rhenium is such a rare and expensive element, it is difficult to find it available on the open market. However, some companies specializing in high-performance materials may be able to provide small quantities of purified rhenium for specific uses. Alternatively, one can turn to specialized material suppliers or research laboratories that may have access to rhenium for scientific or industrial purposes.

In general, rhenium is a very difficult element to find and obtain, but it is crucial for various industrial and scientific applications. Its rarity and high cost make it a very valuable element that requires innovative solutions to be obtained and used effectively.

25.Where to Find Indium

The search for indium metal has been a passion that has involved many mineral enthusiasts and collectors around the world. This mineral is known for its beauty and rarity, and is sought after for its healing and spiritual properties. But where can indium metal be found and how can it be recognized?

Indium metal, also known as indium metal, is a chemical element with the symbol In and atomic number 49. It is a soft and ductile transition metal, silver-white in color, and is mainly used in the production of semiconductors and LCD screens. But it is also a very rare mineral to find in nature, and its physical and chemical properties make it particularly valuable for mineral collectors.

One of the most sought-after areas to find indium metal is in the Ural Mountains region in Russia. This mineral-rich mountain range is known for its mines of precious and rare metals, and indium metal is no exception. Numerous mines in the region extract this valuable mineral, which is then sold on the international market.

Other places where indium metal can be found include China, Japan, Bolivia, and Canada. In particular, Bolivia is one of the main sources of this mineral, with active mines producing a significant amount of indium metal every year. Canada also has several indium metal mines, especially in the Rocky Mountains region and in the province of Newfoundland and Labrador.

But how can indium metal be recognized once found? This mineral is often confused with other similar metals, such as silver and lead. However, indium metal has some distinctive characteristics that make it easily recognizable. For example, it has a characteristic silver-white color, and its surface can be shiny and reflective.

Additionally, it has a soft and ductile texture, making it easily workable.

For mineral collectors and geology enthusiasts, finding and owning a sample of indium metal can be a true fortune. This mineral is particularly coveted for its rarity and intrinsic value, and many seek to add a specimen to their collection. However, it is important to be mindful of local laws and regulations regarding mineral exploration and collection to avoid legal issues.

Indium metal is a rare and precious mineral that can be found in various parts of the world, but mainly in the mines of the Ural Mountains in Russia, Bolivia, Canada, China, and Japan. Its beauty and physical properties make it highly sought after among collectors and mineral enthusiasts, and its rarity makes it a true treasure to possess. If you are interested in finding indium metal, be sure to conduct thorough research on extraction locations and to respect local laws regarding mineral exploration.

Index